Travel
Adventures

Banff
National Park

Area

Dona Herweck Rice

Contributing Author

Alison S. Marzocchi, Ph.D.

Consultant

Colleen Pollitt, M.A.Ed.
Math Support Teacher
Howard County Public Schools

Publishing Credits

Rachelle Cracchiolo, M.S.Ed., *Publisher*
Conni Medina, M.A.Ed., *Editor in Chief*
Dona Herweck Rice, *Series Developer*
Emily R. Smith, M.A.Ed., *Series Developer*
Diana Kenney, M.A.Ed., NBCT, *Content Director*
Stacy Monsman, M.A., *Editor*
Michelle Jovin, M.A., *Associate Editor*
Fabiola Sepulveda, *Graphic Designer*

Image Credits: p.12 wwing/iStock; p.13 (top right) Whyte Museum of the Canadian Rockies, Round family fonds (V547/II/D/pa-8); p.15 (top right) NASA Earth Observatory/ Jesse Allen/Courtesy of the NASA EO-1 team; p.16 Neale Clark/robertharding/Newscom; p.17 (bottom) Songquan Deng/Shutterstock; p.22 Jeff Whyte/Shutterstock; p.23 (top) Jeff Whyte/iStock; p.23 (bottom) Chantal de Bruijne/Shutterstock; p.29 (bottom) Creative Family/iStock; all other images Shutterstock and/or iStock.

Library of Congress Cataloging-in-Publication Data

Names: Rice, Dona, author.
Title: Banff National Park area / Dona Herweck Rice.
Description: Huntington Beach, CA : Teacher Created Materials, 2019. |
  Series: Travel adventures | Includes index. | Audience: Grade 4 to 6. |
  Identifiers: LCCN 2018047792 (print) | LCCN 2018051757 (ebook) | ISBN
  9781425855338 (eBook) | ISBN 9781425858896 (pbk.)
Subjects: LCSH: Banff National Park (Alta.)--Juvenile literature.
Classification: LCC F1079.B5 (ebook) | LCC F1079.B5 R53 2019 (print) | DDC
  971.23/32--dc23
LC record available at https://lccn.loc.gov/2018047792

Teacher Created Materials

5301 Oceanus Drive
Huntington Beach, CA 92649-1030
www.tcmpub.com

ISBN 978-1-4258-5889-6
© 2019 Teacher Created Materials, Inc.
Printed in Malaysia
Thumbprints.21254

Table of Contents

Arrival

"Gross," Lila hissed under her breath, slowly **elongating** the final *s* beneath her curled lips.

"What?" Hector wanted to know, **bounding** up enthusiastically to look over his sister's shoulder.

"That!" Lila directed, pointing at the mound of animal poop she'd nearly stepped in. *What was so great about Banff National Park?* Lila thought. She never even wanted to go on this stupid trip, but her parents had dragged her to this cold and faraway place anyway. It was supposed to be summertime, but she was shivering from the frigid air in the mountain range. She should have been lounging by the swimming pool under the sizzling summer sun! Everything here was Canadian wilderness, but she just wanted to lie back on a sandy California beach. And there was animal poop right in front of her—which her weird brother was now investigating up close!

"Oh, man, I think that's bear poop!" Hector shouted. "Cool! I wonder where the bear went?"

"I *so* don't want to know that answer," Lila said, looking over her shoulder with a glimmer of worry in her eyes. More than anything, she did not want to get up close and personal with a grizzly bear and meet her doom while on vacation! How could Hector be so excited when bears were running loose?

GROUP ACCESS   ACCÈS EN GROUPE
☐ is mandatory   ☐ obligatoire
☑ is recommended   ☑ recommendé

GROUP ACCESS means travel in a tight group of 4 or more for safety.

When GROUP ACCESS is mandatory, you must travel in a group of 4 or more BY LAW.

Anyone not complying with minimum group size may be charged and subject to a court appearance and maximum fine of $5,000.

Grizzly bears are an important part of the Rocky Mountain ecosystem.

ACCÈS EN GROUPE veut dire que pour des raisons de sécurité il faut se déplacer en groupe serré de 4 personnes au moins

Lorsque l'ACCÈS EN GROUPE est obligatoire, il faut se déplacer en groupe de 4 personnes au moins, SELON LA LOI.

Toute personne qui ne se conforme pas aux directives concernant le nombre minimal de personnes dans un groupe, pourrait être inculpée, citée en justice et sera passible d'une amende allant jusqu'à 5 000 $.

Les ours grizzly constituent un élément important de l'écosystème des Rocheuses.

a hiking trail in Banff National Park

Since they had **disembarked** the plane in Calgary in southern Alberta, Canada, Lila was not a happy kid. She missed her home, her friends, and her pet Chihuahua, Bruno. More than anything, she missed walking down a street free of bear poop!

Lila's parents had been planning this trip for months, saying it was on their bucket list. Well, they could keep their buckets! Lila had repeatedly tried to convince them that the family should vacation at the beach this summer. But instead, they wound up here in the Canadian Rockies doing…who knows what people do here? Lila knew this trip was a terrible idea. Her traitor of a brother, on the other hand, let their parents convince him that Banff would be a great adventure, and he was excited to explore the lakes and trails. He even put together a family **itinerary**! Now, Lila was headed for several days of this stinking "great" outdoors.

"Come on, Lila, let's get this party started!" Hector yelled from the hotel doorway.

"Coming," Lila moaned, dragging her suitcase behind her. This trip would definitely be no fun at all.

Lila waits at the airport.

A ranger wants to estimate the total area of Banff National Park. But the shape of the park is unfamiliar—it's definitely not a shape she studied in math class! First, she divides the park into rectangles. Then, she calculates the areas of the rectangles. Finally, she finds the sum of the areas to estimate the total area of the park.

1. How can you tell whether the ranger's estimate is greater or less than the actual total area of the park?

2. What strategies could the ranger use to make an estimate that is closer to the actual total area?

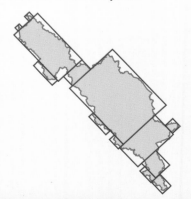

Taking It All In

The family had checked into the hotel just in time for dinner. They were all so exhausted that they ordered room service, watched television, and fell asleep during the credits. But when they woke up the next morning, they were ready for their adventures to begin! Well…everyone was ready except Lila. She was restless all night and was certain the day—in fact, the whole trip—would be a disaster.

"Come on, Lila, stop dragging your feet! This vacation is going to be awesome!" Hector shouted as he bounded around the room, collecting his jacket and a bundle of maps. *Nine-year-old brothers never stop*, Lila thought.

"Hector, slow down!" his mother chided, adding with a laugh, "You'll jump your way right through the floor."

"What's first on our itinerary, son?" Hector's dad asked, handing his son the carefully graphed and illustrated paper Hector had prepared.

"We'll start with a look at all of Banff in just one view," Hector answered mysteriously. Then, grinning, he added, "We're riding the **gondola**!"

Oh, brother. Big deal! Lila thought. But she finished getting ready quickly and departed with her family for their first adventure.

Moraine Lake in Banff

Lila is annoyed by Hector's enthusiasm when they first arrive in Banff. She decides to divide their hotel room in half so they can each have their own area. She creates two plans for dividing the room.

Lila	Hector

Plan 1

Plan 2

1. The dimensions of the hotel room are 8 meters by 4 meters. What are the available areas for Lila and Hector in each plan?

2. Which plan do you think Lila should choose? How can she convince Hector to agree with the plan?

Overhead and All Around

Since they were up so early, the family was among the first in line for the gondola, and they were glad they were because the line rapidly filled up behind them! *People seem to think this gondola thing is a good idea*, Lila thought.

Soon enough, they were in their own cart and lifting off the ground, headed above the trees. Unthinking, Lila caught her breath. It was beautiful—more beautiful than she had imagined. Suddenly aware of the look on her face, Lila quickly changed her expression to **neutral** as her dad asked, "What do you think, Lila?"

"Yeah, it's pretty, I guess," she answered **nonchalantly**.

entrance to the Banff gondolas

"I'll say!" her mother added with wonder. They counted six mountain ranges in their view! The guide had told them they would see everything from an elevation of nearly 7,500 feet (2,300 meters) above sea level. From that viewpoint, they felt as though they could see all of Banff—mountains, trees, lakes, snow, and icecaps. Bow Valley spread out before them, green and breathtaking. Without knowing it, Lila sighed and smiled. Her parents, catching a glimpse, winked at each other over Lila's head.

LET'S EXPLORE MATH

About 4 passengers can fit on a Banff gondola. Imagine that each person needs about 1.2 square meters of floor space. What is the approximate area of the floor space of the gondola? Draw a diagram to support your answer.

The gondola ride was a hit, and the day just got better from there. The gondola took them to Sulphur Mountain where the family stood on the observation deck to look across Bow Valley and Lake Minnewanka. Near them, bighorn sheep **lolled** around the gondola terminal.

"What did I tell you? This is pretty great, right?" Hector asked his big sister.

Lila read hope and expectation in his eyes. She smiled. "Yeah, bud. It's not bad."

Sulphur Mountain observation deck

the Sulphur Mountain
Cosmic Ray Station

Norman Sanson

The family left the deck to walk along another trail. It led them straight to an old weather **observatory**. Lila learned that a **meteorologist** named Norman Sanson had climbed Sulphur Mountain more than a thousand times between 1903 and 1931 to get weather data. This was long before there was a gondola to take him there. The hike up the mountain took him several hours each way.

Lila also learned about the Cosmic Ray Station, which was founded at Sulphur Mountain in 1956. It was one of nine stations across Canada. The stations were built for collecting **geophysical** data. During one year, many countries took part in this data collection. The Sulphur Mountain station stayed in operation until 1978. Now, it is a national landmark.

Lake of the Water Spirit

The next day, the family followed Hector's itinerary and headed to Lake Minnewanka to rent a motorboat. The lake was the largest one in all of Banff National Park, and it certainly was impressive to see up close! Lila's mom had grown up around boats, so she piloted them through the waters. The colors of the lake were striking blues and greens. Tree-covered mountains tipped with snow surrounded Lake Minnewanka. Even in the middle of summer, the mountains had plenty of snow! The name of the lake, Lila learned, means "Lake of the Water Spirit," and it was easy to see why. It almost seemed alive as it glistened and shimmered in the sunlight.

After dropping off the boat, the family splashed along the shore, and Lila and Hector decided to jump in for a swim. Then, they put on their shoes to walk around the rocky beach. Lila was tempted to put a couple of interesting rocks in her pocket, but she knew the first rule of nature: take only pictures, leave only footprints. She sighed. Banff was growing on her.

boats on Lake Minnewanka

LET'S EXPLORE MATH

A ranger wants to estimate the area of the park that is occupied by Lake Minnewanka.

1. Use the map and tracing paper to draw Lake Minnewanka. Then, decompose your drawing into rectangles and triangles the ranger could use to estimate its area.

2. How could you convince the ranger that your drawing will help form an accurate estimate?

Lake Minnewanka, as seen from space

Lake Minnewanka

More Than Can Be Seen

The family completed their trip to Sulphur Mountain with a relaxing stop at Banff Upper Hot Springs. They decided to spend the next day just lounging around the hotel pool and biking through the immediate neighborhood. It was a fun and simple day with some Banff beauty thrown in.

During dinner, they looked over Hector's itinerary, and it soon became clear that he had planned much more for them than they could squeeze into their time frame. So they decided to **prioritize**. Dad wanted to see Athabasca Falls, but Hector pointed out that it was in neighboring Jasper National Park. Mom wanted to see beautiful Bow Lake and the Columbia Icefield. The ice field was exactly that: a big field of glacial ice. They sounded wonderful, but there was probably not enough time to see them during this visit.

"Hey, I know where we should go!" Hector cried. "Last night, I read about Lake Louise and the St. Agnes Trail. There is even a teahouse up there, Mom, and a mountaintop called the Big Beehive! We have to go—okay?"

The family agreed, and that was their next day's adventure.

Banff Upper Hot Springs pool

People drive alongside Bow Lake.

a snow coach on the Columbia Icefield

Louise and Agnes

First thing in the morning, the family drove out to Lake Louise. They were eager to see it for themselves. They had read that Lake Louise is 1.5 miles (2.4 kilometers) long and 0.75 miles (1.2 kilometers) wide. It is deeper than 220 ft. (67 m). Bordered by glacier ice and winter snow, the emerald-green water reaches a high temperature of about 39 degrees Fahrenheit (4 degrees Celsius).

The hotel staff warned them that parking at the lake filled up quickly, but they were lucky enough to nab one of the last available spaces. The family grabbed their hiking gear and walked to the lake's eastern shore. Turning the corner, they were **awestruck**. They had seen the photos online, but nothing prepared them for the beauty that is Lake Louise.

"Wow," Mom and Dad murmured together.

"I didn't know water could be this color!" Hector added.

Lila said nothing. She simply stared and then grabbed her smartphone. If ever there was a selfie moment, this was it!

"Maybe this trip isn't so bad, eh, Lila?" Mom asked, **diplomatically** avoiding mention of Lila's **unabashed** grin.

"Well…maybe not," Lila agreed **sheepishly**.

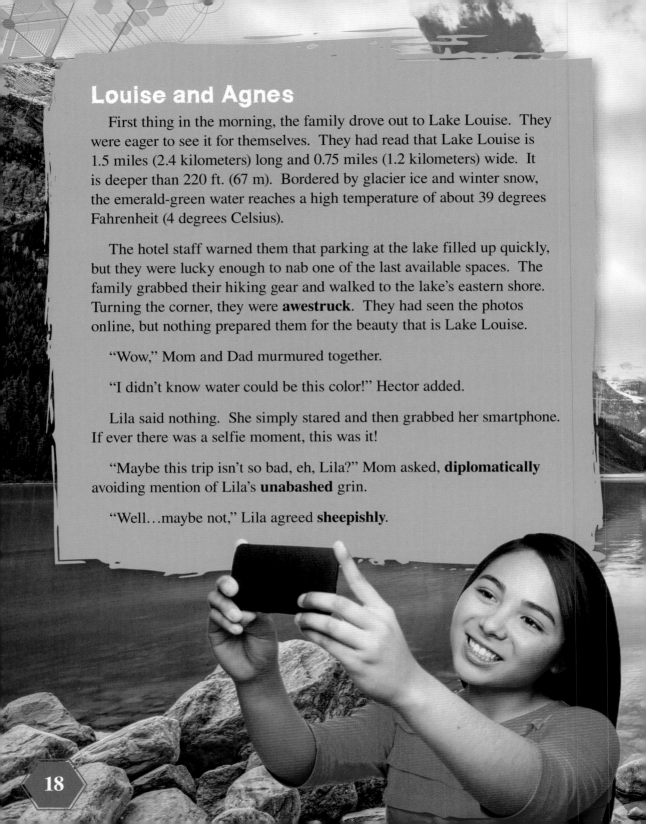

Lake Louise is famous for its emerald-colored water.

Lake Louise, as seen from the Lakeview Trail

LET'S EXPLORE MATH

Lila's family reads that Lake Louise is 2.4 kilometers long and 1.2 kilometers wide. If Lila uses a rectangle to estimate, what is the area of the park occupied by the lake?

Next, the family decided to start hiking to the Lake Agnes Tea House. They followed a winding footpath through the forest and around the lake. Lila was nervous about running into a bear there, but the heavy traffic on the trail soon calmed her nerves. Bears avoided crowds of people—right?

Along the trail, the family was delighted to spot Mirror Lake. Its green waters stood still in the sunlight, reflecting the surrounding landscape as a mirror would. Hector could not help himself; he skipped a stone right through the still image, making it ripple. Soon, the whole family was skipping rocks. Lila managed a double skip, but Hector beat her with a triple!

"I'm hungry!" Hector **interjected** mid-skip, and everyone agreed they were too. They continued their hike, finally making it to the long stairway below the Lake Agnes Tea House. It was a café right in the middle of the wilderness! They ordered snacks and fueled up for their last big push to the Big Beehive mountaintop. From its **vantage point**, they looked down on the majestic beauty of Lake Louise, completely exhausted but agreeing their effort was worth the view. And for Lila, it was time for another selfie!

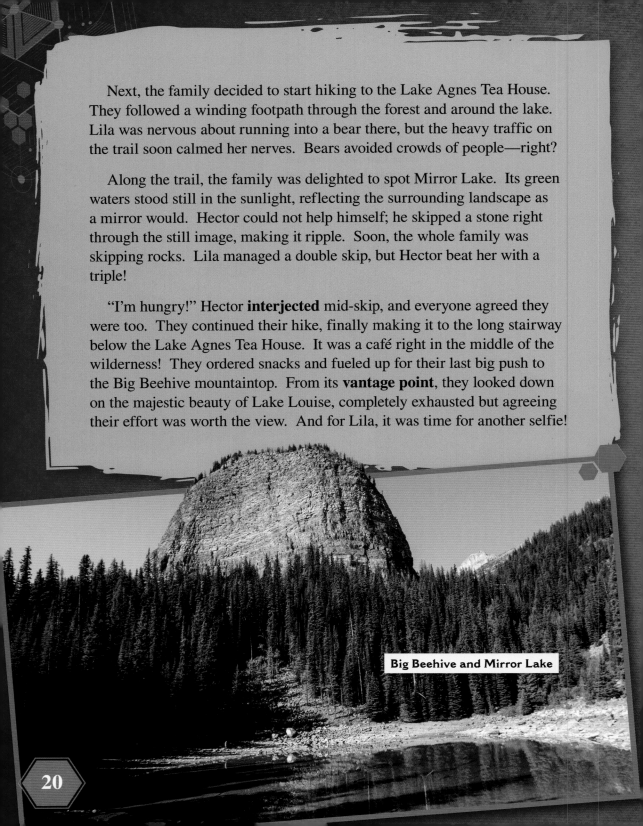

Big Beehive and Mirror Lake

Lake Louise, as seen from Big Beehive

The sides of the Lake Agnes Tea House are open, so guests can see breathtaking views while they enjoy their meals. The front of the tea house is a pentagon, but the horizontal and vertical beams divide it into smaller polygons.

1. Use the dimensions to find the area of the front-facing side of the teahouse. Explain your strategy.

2. Describe how you can use a different set of polygons to find the area of the front-facing side of the teahouse.

6 ft.
3 ft.
7 ft.
12 ft.
12 ft.

Around Town

After leaving Lake Louise, Lila convinced everyone to visit Radium Hot Springs outside the park. It was bigger and less crowded than Banff Upper Hot Springs. It was an excellent way to finish their day, and it definitely earned them a good night's sleep! They woke up the next morning refreshed and ready to go—but instead of heading into the wilderness, they decided to explore what the town of Banff had to offer.

First, they strolled down Banff Avenue, eating breakfast at one of the restaurants and making some purchases in the shops along the road. Lila and Hector had allowance money to spend, and it was burning holes in their pockets. Hector bought a souvenir slingshot, but Lila could not decide what to get.

"You'll know when you see it," Mom encouraged her.

Turning off Banff Avenue, they explored some of the side streets. Noticing the street names, Hector cried, "Hey! These are named after all the animals I've seen around here. There's Caribou, and that one is Lynx. Oh, and this one is for you, Lila—Bear Street!"

"Ugh! No way am I going down that street," Lila scowled, turning in the opposite direction.

Radium Hot Spings

GRIZZLY HOUSE STEAKS

207

LICENCED RESTAURANT
GRIZZLY HOUSE
STEAK & CHEESE FONDUE
BUFFALO & CARIBOU SERVED
バッファロ・肉,鹿肉 とうございます

ENTRANCE

Wolf St

People shop on Banff Avenue.

No sooner had Lila turned than she froze in her tracks, stopping so fast that Hector collided into her. Dad snapped, "Lila, what are you doing?" but then he saw what she saw. Mom saw it, too, and gasped. Lila wanted to run, but she could not will her feet to move. Walking down the middle of the street was a real, live, brown and bushy grizzly bear!

Everyone stared, mouths hanging open. The bear glanced at them but just turned away, slowly and steadily walking down the street and into a wooded grove at the end of the lane. As it passed, Lila noticed its heavy **haunches**, its thick coat, and its powerful limbs—but more than anything, she noticed its beauty. Of all the wonders she had seen in Banff, it was absolutely the most wonderful. As she watched it walk into the grove, she realized the most dominant feeling she had felt was awe. She had seen a bear up close and personal, and it was one of the most beautiful and amazing things she had ever seen.

LET'S EXPLORE MATH

Imagine that the grizzly bear spotted in town has a minor injury. The staff at a local wildlife sanctuary wants to help it heal before releasing it back into the wild. It is recommended that captive bears have at least 850 square meters of space. The sanctuary has this enclosure available. Prove whether it is large enough to house the bear.

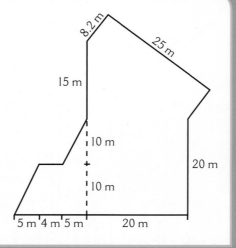

The Great Outdoors

It took the family a minute to shake themselves from their trances. But Mom broke the spell first, stammering, "Did we just see what I think we saw?"

"Uh…yep, I think we did," Dad answered, astonished.

Lila had a sudden idea. "Can we go back to that last shop, Mom? I know what I want to get." Minutes later, she exited the shop, wearing her special purchase—a brightly colored T-shirt reading Banff National Park. Pictured on the shirt was a mountaintop with a hiker and a bear hiking across it together. Lila smiled again. Yes, Banff was definitely growing on her.

For the rest of their vacation, Lila snapped photographs everywhere, especially of wildlife. Her fear was replaced with wonder, and she was **mesmerized** with the range of nature's beauties that were visible in this one breathtaking corner of the Canadian Rockies. Sure, a beach vacation still sounded great, but she would not change her Banff experience—and her moment with a bear—for the sandiest beach or waviest shore.

The great outdoors? Yes, Lila thought, they really are.

Lila admires the sunset at Banff.

Mount Chephren in Banff

grizzly bear in Banff

Problem Solving

Lila ended up having more fun on her family vacation than she anticipated. She explored nature and the town of Banff. She decided that the great outdoors could be part of her dream vacation.

Think about your dream vacation. Does it include natural features, such as hiking trails and lakes? Or, does it include human-made fun, such as water parks and roller coasters? Turn that dream into reality by designing a vacation village.

Draw a rectangle like the one on page 29. Use it as an outline for the design of your vacation village. You may include whatever vacation features you like within your design, but you must follow these parameters:

❏ Include at least four features with different shapes.

❏ Cover the entire area of the village.

❏ Label the dimensions of each feature.

❏ Find the area of each feature.

Then, respond to the prompts to summarize your design.

1. List all the features in your vacation village.

2. Calculate the areas of all the features.

3. Prove that the sum of all the areas is equal to the area of the village's outline.

100 km

50 km

Glossary

awestruck—inspired or filled with wonder

bounding—leaping and jumping

diplomatically—done with an effort to maintain a good relationship

disembarked—left a boat or plane

elongating—making something longer than usual

geophysical—geology relating to the earth and its atmosphere

gondola—an enclosed cart that hangs from a cable to transport passengers

haunches—the upper parts of animals' legs

interjected—interrupted

itinerary—a plan for places to visit on a trip

lolled—sat in a relaxed way

mesmerized—very interested or amazed

meteorologist—a scientist who studies weather

neutral—without emotion or opinion

nonchalantly—with a sense of calm

observatory—a viewing station

prioritize—to organize things in a way so that the most important thing will be done first

sheepishly—with a sense of embarrassment

unabashed—not embarrassed or ashamed

vantage point—a position from which something can be viewed well

Index

Answer Key

Let's Explore Math

page 7

1. greater than; The area of each rectangle is greater than the area of the park it contains.

2. Strategies may include using rectangles that are larger and smaller than the areas they contain, smaller rectangles that fit more closely, or a combination of rectangles and triangles.

page 9

1. Lila: 16 sq. m; Hector: 16 sq. m

2. Answers will vary. Example: *I think Lila should use Plan 1 because it will be easier to make the dividing line. Lila can show Hector that both plans give each of them the same area.*

page 11

4.8 sq. m; Diagrams will vary. Example:

1.2 sq. m	1.2 sq. m
1.2 sq. m	1.2 sq. m

page 15

1. Drawings should show rectangles and triangles that do not overlap and that closely cover the area of the lake.

2. Answers will vary. Example: *My drawing uses rectangles and triangles that closely fit the area of the lake. The estimate will be less than the actual since my shapes are smaller than the areas they cover.*

page 19

2.88 sq. km

page 21

1. 312 sq. ft.; Strategies should include using rectangles and triangles to find areas of smaller shapes and finding the sum of the areas.

2. Strategies should include using a different set of polygons than those used in question 1. Area is still 312 sq. ft.

page 24

Yes; The total area is 895 sq. m.

Problem Solving

Designs should include 4 differently shaped features covering the entire rectangle, with dimensions and areas labeled.

1. Lists should include names of features.

2. Areas will vary.

3. Answers should prove that the sum of the areas is equal to 5,000 sq. km.